**What kind of motorbike does Santa ride?
A Holly Davidson**

What beats his chest and swings from
Christmas cake to Christmas cake?
Tarzipan

What do you call a bunch of chess players bragging
about their games in a hotel lobby?
Chess nuts boasting in an open foyer

What's Santa Claus's favourite type of potato chip?
Crisp Pringles

What is white and minty?
A polo bear

What do you get if you cross Santa with a detective?
Santa Clues

What do you call Father Christmas at the beach?
Sandy Claus

What do you get if you cross Father Christmas
with a duck?
A Christmas Quacker

What do you get if Santa comes down the chimney
while the fire is still burning?
Crisp Kringle

What is twenty feet tall, has sharp teeth and goes
Ho Ho Ho?
Tyranno-santas Rex!

Can Santa's reindeer fly higher than a 15-story building?
Of course they can, buildings can't fly at all..

Where do you find flying reindeer?
Wherever you left them

Which one of Santa's reindeer has the worst manners?
Rude-olph

What does Rudolph want for Christmas?
A pony sleigh station

What goes Ho, Ho, Swoosh! Ho, Ho, Swoosh?
Santa caught in a revolving door

What's red & white and red & white and red & white?
Santa rolling down a hill

What do you call a kitty on the beach on Christmas morning?
Sandy Claws

What do you call a female elf?
A shelf

What goes oh, oh, oh?
Santa reversing his sleigh

What does Father Christmas like to get when he goes to the donut shop?
A jolly roll

What does Santa like to have for breakfast?
Mistle-toast

What is an elf's favourite sport?
North-pole vault

What do they sing at a snowman's birthday party?
Freeze a jolly good fellow

What happened to the man who stole an
Advent Calendar?
He got 25 days

Why did the turkey join the band?
Because it had the drumsticks

How does Good King Wenceslas like his pizzas?
Deep pan, crisp and even

What carol is sung in the desert?
O camel ye faithful

What does Miley Cyrus have at Christmas?
Twerky

Where do reindeer go if they lose a tail?
The retail store

Which athlete is warmest in winter?
A long jumper

Why don't you ever see Father Christmas in the hospital?
Because he has private elf care

Why did Santa's little helper go in for counselling?
He had low elf esteem

What are the best Christmas sweaters made from?
Fleece Navidad

What do you give a modern dog for Christmas?
A smart bone

What do Santa's little helpers learn at school?
The elf-abet

Why did no one bid for Rudolph and Blitzen
at the auction?
Because they were two deer

Why couldn't the skeleton go to the Christmas party?
He had nobody to go with

Who delivers presents to cats?
Santa Paws

How does Darth Vader enjoy his Christmas Turkey?
On the dark side

What do monkeys sing at Christmas?
Jungle bells

What is the most competitive season?
Win-ter

I noticed the computer department started putting up their Christmas decorations.
IT's beginning to look a lot like Christmas

Who does Santa Claus work for?
He's elf employed

What did Santa give his depressed elf friend for Christmas?
An elf-help book

Why did Frosty the Snowman want a divorce?
His wife was a total flake

What did the salt say to the pepper?
Seasons greetings

Why shouldn't you lend money to elves?
When they pay you back they're always short

Why shouldn't you trust snowmen?
They are always up to snow good

Where does Santa store his suit?
In his Claus-et

Why do reindeer wear bells?
Because their horns don't work

What did Mr. and Mrs. Claus name their daughter?
Mary Christmas

Knock Knock!
Who's there?
Snow
Snow who?
Snow business like show business!

Knock knock!
Who's there?
Hanna
Hanna who?
Hanna partridge in a pear tree!

Knock knock!
Who's there?
The Holly
The Holly who?
The Holly-days are coming!

Knock knock!
Who's there?
Mary
Mary who?
Mary Christmas!

Knock, knock!
Who's there?
Howard
Howard who?
Howard you like to sing Christmas carols with me?

Knock, knock
Who's there?
Honda
Honda who?
Honda first day of Christmas my true love sent to me

Knock, knock!
Who's there?
Oakham
Oakham who?
Oakham all ye faithful

Knock, knock!
Who's there?
Ima
Ima who?
Ima dreaming of a white Christmas

Why are Christmas trees so fond of the past?
Because the present's beneath them

How does Christmas Day end?
With the letter Y

Who hides in the bakery at Christmas?
A mince spy

Want to hear a joke about wrapping paper?
It's tearable

What is Santa's favourite model railroad scale?
HO

What do snowmen eat for lunch?
Icebergers

What does Father Christmas do when his elves misbehave?
He gives them the sack

Why are Christmas trees bad at knitting?
Because they always drop their needles

What do you call a blind reindeer?
No eye deer

What do you call a reindeer with no eyes, that's not moving?
Still no eye deer

Why do birds fly south in the winter?
Because it's too far to walk

How many letters are in the alphabet at Christmas?
25. There's no-el

What did the farmer get for Christmas?
A cowculator

What did one snowman say to the other snowman?
Can you smell carrots?

Which side of a turkey has the most feathers?
The outside

What do you sing at a snowman's birthday party?
Freeze a jolly good fellow

Who delivers presents to baby sharks at Christmas?
Santa Jaws

What is the most popular Christmas wine?
I don't like sprouts

What kind of music do elves listen to?
Wrap

What do reindeer put on their Christmas trees?
Hornaments

What happened when Santa got stuck in a chimney?
He felt Claus-trophobic

How does Santa keep track of all the fireplaces he's visited?
He keeps a logbook

Why does Santa have three gardens?
So he can hoe hoe hoe

Why does your nose get tired in winter?
It runs all day

What did the Princess say when her photos didn't arrive for Christmas?
One day my prints will come

Why was the snowman rummaging through a bag of carrots?
He was picking his nose

What do you call a bankrupt Santa?
Saint Nickel-less

What do you call a man who claps at Christmas?
Santapplause

What type of Shoes does Santa wear when he travels on a train?
Platforms

Which is the musical elf's favourite reindeer?
Dancer

What do elves post on Social Media?
Elf-ies

What do vampires sing on New Year's Eve?
Auld Fang Syne

How does Rudolph know when Christmas is coming?
He looks at his calen-deer

What is the best Christmas present in the world?
A broken drum, you just can't beat it

What do you call a snowman that can walk?
Snow-mobile

What did Santa say to the smoker?
Please don't smoke, it's bad for my elf

Why are Christmas trees so bad at sewing?
They always drop their needles

Did Rudolph go to school?
No. He was elf-taught

What do you get when you cross a
snowman with a vampire?
Frostbite

What do snowmen wear on their heads?
Ice caps

Knock, knock!
Who's there?
A Wayne
A Wayne who?
A Wayne in a manger

Knock, knock!
Who's there?
Dexter
Dexter who?
Dexter halls with boughs of holly

Knock, knock!
Who's there?
Olive
Olive who?
Olive the other reindeer
used to laugh and call him names

Knock, knock!
Who's there?
Oh, Chris
Oh, Chris who?
Oh Christmas tree, Oh Christmas tree

Knock, knock!
Who's there?
Freeze
Freeze who?
Freeze a jolly good fellow

Knock, knock!
Who's there?
Elf
Elf who?
Elf me wrap this present

Knock, knock!
Who's there?
Yule
Yule who?
Yule be sorry if you don't Holly up and Elf me wrap this present!

Knock, knock!
Who's there?
Luke
Luke who?
Luke at all those presents

What did the snowflake say to the fallen leaf?
You are so last season

How did Santa describe the elf who
refused to take a bath?
He's elfully smelly

How do elves get to the top floor of Santa's workshop?
They use the elfalator

Why did Santa go to the doctor?
For an elf check

What did the sea say to Santa?
Nothing, it just waved

How you can tell that Santa is real?
You can always sense his presents

What do ducks do before their Christmas dinner?
They pull their quackers

What goes Ho, Ho, Ho, thump?
Santa laughing his head off

What is Santa's favourite place to deliver presents?
Idaho-ho-ho

Why does Santa go down the chimney on Christmas Eve?
Because it soots him

What does Santa pay every month?
Jingle Bills

What do you call Santa's little helpers?
Subordinate clauses

Why is Santa so good at karate?
Because he has a black belt

What do you call a man who claps at Christmas?
Santapplause

What is Santa's favourite Railroad?
The Santa Fe

How much does Santa have to pay to park his sleigh?
Nothing. It's on the house

Where do elves go to dance?
Christmas Balls

What do elves eat for breakfast?
Either Frosted Flakes or Ice Crispies

Who brings fizzy drinks on Christmas?
Fanta Claus

What do you call a frozen elf hanging from the ceiling?
An elfcicle

What do you call an elf wearing ear muffs?
Anything you like, they can't hear you

What brand of cars do elves like?
Toy-ota and Elfa-romeo

Who is the king of Santa's rock and roll helpers?
Elfis (Thank you, thank you very much!)

What do Christmas trees wear at the pool?
Swimming trunks

Who is Santa Claus married to?
Mary Christmas

What do you call Santa when he stops moving?
Santa Pause

What is the name of Santa's meanest reindeer?
Olive. Olive the other reindeer,
used to laugh and call him names..

How long do a reindeers legs have to be?
Long enough so they can touch the ground!

How many Christmas trees can you plant in an empty field?
Only one because then the field isn't empty anymore

Why don't reindeer like picnics?
Because of all their ant-lures

What's the best Christmas gift for someone
who has everything?
A burglar alarm

What do angry mice send each other at Christmas?
Cross mouse cards

What do you get if you eat Christmas decorations?
Tinsilitis

Why don't penguins drive the sleigh?
Because they can't reach the pedals

What's green, covered in tinsel and goes ribbet ribbet?
A mistle-toad

Which famous playwright was terrified of Christmas?
Noël Coward

What did the stamp say to the Christmas card?
Stick with me and we'll go places

What did Father Christmas do when he went speed dating?
He pulled a cracker

How did Mary and Joseph know that Jesus was 7lb 6oz when he was born?
They had a weigh in a manger

Why is it getting harder to buy Advent calendars?
Because their days are numbered

Knock, knock!
Who's there?
Doughnut
Doughnut who?
Doughnut open until Christmas

Knock, knock!
Who's there?
Pikachu
Pikachu who?
Pikachu Christmas presents and you'll be in trouble

Knock, knock!
Who's there?
Snow
Snow who?
Snow time to waste. It's almost Christmas

Knock, knock!
Who's there?
Claus
Claus who?
Claus this door again and I won't be happy

Knock, knock!
Who's there?
Harry
Harry who?
Harry up and open your gift

Knock, knock!
Who's there?
Norway
Norway who?
Norway am I kissing anyone under the mistletoe

Knock, Knock!
Who's there?
Izzin
Izzin who?
Izzin Christmas fun?

Knock, Knock!
Who's there?
Ya
Ya who?
Someone's excited for Christmas

What do you get when you cross a deer with rain?
A raindeer

What game do reindeers play at sleepovers?
Truth or deer

Where do Santa's reindeer stop for coffee?
Star bucks

What do you call a scary reindeer?
A Cari-BOO

What's worse than Rudolph with a runny nose?
Frosty the snowman with a hot flush

Why did the reindeer cross the road?
To deliver presents

What is a reindeer's favourite Christmas song?
We wish you a Merry Christmoose

Why did Rudolph get in trouble for his report card?
Because he went down in history

Why did the Rudolph cross the road?
Because he was tied to the chicken

What does Santa clean his sleigh with?
Santatizer

Why did the turkey cross the road?
Because it was the chicken's day off

What happened to the turkey at Christmas?
It got gobbled

How did the two rival Christmas trees get along?
They signed a peace tree-ty

How does a snowman get to work?
By icicle

What do snowmen eat for lunch?
Iceburgers or Brrrr-itos

When is a boat just like snow?
When it's adrift

What did one snowman say to the other?
I couldn't hear them, so I have snow-idea

Where do snowmen keep their money?
In a snowbank

What do snowmen like to do on the weekend?
Chill

What do you call a snowman who
vacations in the tropics?
A puddle

What did the green present say to the red present?
Nothing. Presents can't talk

What did Adam say on the day before Christmas?
"It's Christmas, Eve!"

Why do cats take so long to wrap presents?
They want them to be purr-fect

What type of bug can't remember the words to carols?
A humbug

How do sheep in Spain say Merry Christmas?
Fleece Navidad

How did Scrooge win the football game?
The ghost of Christmas passed

What made Father Christmas have itchy skin?
Excemas

Why do ghosts live in the fridge?
Because it's cool

What did the beaver say to the Christmas Tree?
Nice gnawing you

What do you get if you cross a
Christmas tree with an apple?
A pineapple

What happened when the snowgirl fell out
with the snowboy?
She gave him the cold shoulder

What is an art museum called when it is
made out of an igloo?
The Ig-Louvre

Why do Christmas trees make such wonderful pets?
They have a great bark, but wooden bite

What do fish sing at Christmas time?
Christmas Corals

What did the Christmas tree say to the ornament?
Quit hanging around

What is a Christmas Tree's favourite candy?
Ornamints

What do you get when you cross a pine cone and a polar bear?
A fur tree

Why wouldn't the cat climb the Christmas tree?
It was afraid of the bark

Why didn't the rope get any Christmas presents?
It was knotty

What did one mince pie say to the other?
Nothing. Mince pies can't talk

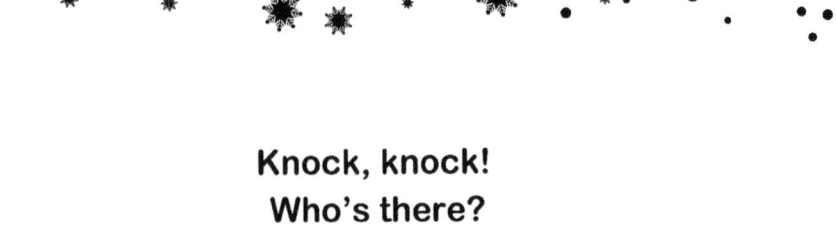

Knock, knock!
Who's there?
Snow
Snow who?
Snow use. I've forgotten my name again

Knock, knock!
Who's there?
Alaska
Alaska who?
Alaska again. What do you want for Christmas?

Knock, knock!
Who's there?
Wanda
Wanda who?
Wanda know what you're getting for Christmas?

Knock, knock!
Who's there?
Anita
Anita who?
Anita put the Christmas tree up

Knock, knock!
Who's there?
Wooden shoe
Wooden shoe who?
Wooden shoe like to know what I got you for Christmas

Knock, knock!
Who's there?
Rabbit
Rabbit who?
Rabbit up carefully please, the present is fragile

Knock, knock!
Who's there?
Kanye
Kanye who?
Kanye help me untangle my Christmas lights?

Knock, knock!
Who's there?
Tank
Tank who?
Tank you for my Christmas present

What do crackers, fruitcake and nuts remind me of?
You!

Where does Mistletoe go to become famous?
Holly wood

What's the best thing to put into a Christmas Cake?
Your teeth

What do you get if you cross a bell with a skunk?
Jingle Smells

Where would you find chili beans?
At the north pole

Why is everyone so thirsty at the north pole?
No well, no well

Why don't penguins fly?
Because they're not tall enough to be pilots

Why do penguins swim in saltwater?
Because pepper makes them sneeze

What did the Gingerbread Man put on his bed?
A cookie sheet

Why did the Gingerbread Man go to the doctors?
Because he felt crummy

What do sheep say at Christmas?
Wool-tide Bleatings or A Merry Christmas to Ewe

Which football team did the baby Jesus support?
Manger-ster United

What type of key do you need for a Nativity play?
A don-key

What do you call a three legged donkey?
A wonky

How did one shepherd make the other shepherd laugh?
He played a sheep trick on him

What did one Angel say to the other?
Halo there

What's the name of the one horse in Jingle Bells?
Bob. (Bells on Bob's tail ring)

Why do mummies like Christmas so much?
Because there's wrapping

Where does Christmas come before Thanksgiving?
In the dictionary

How did the ornament get addicted to Christmas?
He was hooked on trees his whole life

What would you call an elf who just has won the lottery?
Welfy

What's the difference between snowmen and snow women?
Snowballs

What's the difference between a knight and Santa's reindeer?
The knight is slaying the dragon, and the reindeer are dragon the sleigh

What do you call a kid who doesn't believe in Santa?
A rebel without a Claus

What do you call an old snowman?
Water

What's the difference between Batman and the Grinch?
Batman can go into Whoville without Robin

Why did Mary and Joseph have to travel to Bethlehem?
Because they couldn't book a home delivery

What do you call a penguin in the Sahara desert?
Lost

What is a girl snowman called?
A snow-ma'am

I got a Christmas card full of rice in the post today..
I think it was from my Uncle Ben

How did Darth Vader know what Luke Skywalker got for Christmas?
He felt his presents

Why did the Grinch go to Bargain Booze?
He was searching for some holiday spirit

What do elves do after school?
Their gnome work

Why did the snowman turn yellow?
Ask the little dog over there

When is a Christmas dinner bad for your health?
When you're the turkey

Why did Santa cover his guitar in snow?
He wanted to play some cool music

What did one Christmas light say to the other Christmas light?
You light me up

How does a snowman lose weight?
He waits for warmer weather

What is the Grinch's least favourite band?
The Who

What do you get if Santa forgets to wear his undercrackers?
St Nickerless

Knock, knock!
Who's there?
Canoe
Canoe who?
Canoe help me bake some Christmas cookies?

Knock, knock!
Who's there?
Lettuce
Lettuce who?
Lettuce in for some figgy pudding

Knock, knock!
Who's there?
Yule
Yule who?
Yule know when you open the door

Knock, knock!
Who's there?
Snow
Snow who?
Snow one's at the door

Knock, knock!
Who's there?
Elf
Elf who?
Elf I knock again will you let me in?

Knock, knock!
Who's there?
Irish
Irish who?
Irish you a Merry Christmas

Knock, knock!
Who's there?
Ho Ho
Ho Ho who?
Your Santa impression needs a little work

Knock, knock!
Who's there?
Ivana
Ivana who?
Ivana wish you a Merry Christmas.

Who's Rudolph's favourite pop star?
Beyon-sleigh

Which Christmas carol is about an animal with three legs?
Little Wonkey

What do you call a snowman who goes on Love Island?
A melt

How can you keep your home warm this Christmas?
Tinsulation

Why can't the Christmas tree stand up?
It doesn't have legs

Who is Santa's favourite actor?
Willem Dafoe-ho-ho

Who tells the best Christmas jokes?
Reindeer. They sleigh every time

Where do you find reindeer?
In rain clouds

Who is a Christmas tree's favourite singer?
Spruce Springsteen

Where does Santa stay when he goes on holiday?
In a ho-ho-hotel

What does Santa use to bake cakes?
Elf-raising flour

Why don't Santa's reindeer catch a cold?
They have herd immunity

Why is it best to think of last year like a panto?
Because it's behind you

Why wouldn't Ebenezer Scrooge eat at the pasta restaurant?
It cost a pretty penne

Why couldn't Mary and Joseph join the conference call?
There was no Zoom at the inn

Why does Kate Bush need to turn the heating off?
She's running up that bill

Why are Father Christmas and the Grinch not having turkey this year?
Because they've got beef

Why has Santa been banned from sooty chimneys?
Carbon footprints

I have this incredible ability to predict what is inside a wrapped present..
It's a gift

What does Santa use when he goes fishing?
His north pole

Why did Santa get a parking ticket on Christmas eve?
He left his sleigh in a snow parking zone

The Christmas jumper my kids gave me last year kept picking up static electricity..
I took it back and exchanged it for another one..
Free of charge.

Wife: I regret getting you that blender for Christmas.
Me: *sipping toast* Why?

Where does Santa Claus go swimming?
The North Pool

How many chimneys does Santa go down?
Stacks

The only Christmas present that I got this year was
a deck of sticky playing cards.
I find that very hard to deal with

Did you know that Santa actually only had two reindeer?
Rudolph and Olive (the other reindeer)

My friend just won the Tallest
Christmas Tree competition.
I thought to myself, "How can you top that?"

Why is the turkey never hungry at Christmas?
It's stuffed

What's every parent's favourite Christmas Carol?
Silent Night

Children: This turkey tastes like an old sofa
Mum: Well, you asked for something with plenty of stuffing

Where do snowman do their christmas shopping?
On the winternet

What do you get when you cross a snowman with a baker?'
Frosty the Dough-Man

Who does Santa call when his sleigh breaks down?
The Abominable Towman

What is the same size as Santa and yet weighs nothing?
His shadow

What do you call Santa in the South Pole?
A lost Claus

How does Santa take pictures?
With a north pole-aroid

What did Santa say when he won the pan at the raffle?
That's what I call potluck

Why was Christmas dinner awkward?
There was an elf-ant in the room

What did Santa say to his naughty elf?
You're mistle-toeing the line

Knock, knock!
Who's there?
Murray
Murray who?
Murray Christmas to all, and to all a good night

Knock, knock!
Who's there?
Mary and Abby
Mary and Abby who?
Mary Christmas and Abby New Year!

Knock, knock!
Who's there?
Snow
Snow who?
Snowbody home

Knock, knock!
Who's there?
Ida
Ida who?
Ida know but I hope it's Santa

Knock knock!
Who's there?
Ben
Ben who?
Ben thinking about what to get you for Christmas

Knock knock!
Who's there?
Icy
Icy who?
Icy you've been feeling the Christmas presents

Knock knock!
Who's there?
Arthur
Arthur who?
Arthur any mince pies left?

Knock knock!
Who's there?
Heaven
Heaven who?
Heaven seen you since last Christmas

What's Santa's favourite cartoon character?
Chimney Cricket

What do road crews use in the North Pole?
Snow cones

Why were the toys getting stressed out?
Because they were being wound up

What did the Christmas tree wear to stay warm?
A fir coat

Why did the elf clink his wine glass?
To give a mistle-toast

What is Santa's favourite wine?
Prosec-ho-ho-ho

What did the teacher say to her elves?
All line up in jingle file

How did the snow globe feel after the accident?
A little shaken

How did Mr. and Mrs. Claus fall in love?
It was love at frost sight

What did the grumpy sheep say on Christmas?
Baaaaa humbug

Why was it chilly on Christmas morning?
Because it's Decemberrrrr

What do you call a snowman with no arms or legs?
A snowball

What did Santa say to the rowdy elf?
Please don't Claus a scene

How did the elf get out of trouble?
He was saved by the jingle bell

What did the elf use when he broke his leg?
Candy canes

What did the cop say when he caught a
snowman stealing?
Freeze!

What is Santa's favourite candy?
Jolly Ranchers

What did Santa say when his elves hid the toys?
This is snow laughing matter

What did the reindeer say after he
got hit with a snowball?
Yule be sorry

What did Santa say to his elves?
Here's a mistle-token of my appreciation

Why did the branches fall in love?
They had great chemis-tree

Why did the elf look so mad?
He had a resting Grinch face

Why did Mrs. Claus get to help deliver gifts?
She had the final sleigh

What's a child's favourite king at Christmas
A stoc-king

What looks like half a Christmas tree?
The other half

What did the Christmas tree do after its bank closed?
It started its own branch

What goes inside elves' pointy shoes?
Their mistletoes

How did the elf sleep in the fireplace?
Like a log

What's the best way to gain confidence?
Believe in your elf

What do you do if you can't hire a professional?
Do it your elf

What do you get when an elf passes wind?
Jingle smells

Which penguin gave the most presents this year?
Aunt Arctica

Why are turtles so excited for Christmas?
Because they love a good shellebration

What did the lost crab say when he finally made it to Christmas dinner?
Long time no sea

Why are Orcas always the life of the Christmas party?
Because they do a killer whale impression

What does December have that no other month has?
The letter D

How do you make a snowman's bed?
With fresh sheets of ice and a thick blanket of snow

What do you call it when a little snowman has a tantrum?
A meltdown

What kind of robots live at the North Pole?
Snow-bots

How do you protect yourself against angry snowmen?
A hairdryer

Knock knock!
Who's there?
Juicy
Juicy who?
Juicy it's given snow for tomorrow?

Knock knock!
Who's there?
Marv
Marv who?
Marv-elous time of year is Christmas, isn't it?

Knock knock!
Who's there?
Dewey
Dewey who?
Dewey know when Santa is going to be on the roof?

Knock knock!
Who's there?
Shirley
Shirley who?
Shirley you're not taking your
Christmas tree down already?

Knock knock!
Who's there?
Tamara
Tamara who?
Tamara night you know who is coming down the chimney

Knock knock!
Who's there?
Beef
Beef who?
Beef for real, Santa can't possibly have
put you on the nice list

Knock knock!
Who's there?
Candy
Candy who?
Candy really visit all those houses in one night?

Knock knock!
Who's there?
It's Chris
It's Chris who?
It's Christmas!

Why shouldn't you ever owe Santa money?
He snows where you live

What currency does Santa use in the North Pole?
Cold, hard cash

What do you call a person who talks a lot about last Christmas?
Santa-mental

What does Santa say to begin a race?
Ready, set, ho ho ho!

What's red, white, and green?
Santa when he gets travel sick

What does Santa say when he feels sick?
Ho ho no

What's red, white, red, white, red, white, red, white?
Santa rolling down a hill

What kind of salad do they serve at the North Pole?
Iceberg lettuce

What did Santa say to the elves about their tree-decorating skills?
You need to spruce it up

Why did the Christmas tree visit the hospital?
Because it was feeling green

What did the festive Christmas tree say to the sad Christmas tree?
Lighten up

What happens when Christmas trees go numb?
They get pines and needles

Why did the Christmas tree apply for a new job?
It wanted to branch out

What do you call a reindeer with five eyes?
A Reiiiiindeer

Why did the reindeer cross the road?
Because chickens don't live at the North Pole

What do you call a group of reindeer in the desert?
Lost

How do you know if Santa's been in your garden shed?
You've got three extra hoes

What's worse than a reindeer with a cold?
A snowman with a fever

What do you put over a baby reindeer's crib?
A snow-mobile

What's a reindeer's favourite time at school?
Snow-and-tell

What do reindeer like about rainy winter days?
Rein-bows

How do they build skyscrapers at the North Pole?
A crane-deer

What does Santa do when the reindeer fly too fast?
Holds onto the sleigh for deer life

What is Rudolph's favourite sport?
Stable tennis

How did the Gingerbread Man get locked out of his house?
He lost his cook-keys

What is a fruit salad's favourite Christmas carol?
Have Yourself a Berry Little Christmas

What did one cranberry say to the other cranberry?
Tis the season to be jelly

Why do feet make good Christmas presents?
They're great stocking fillers

What do snowmen call their kids?
Chill-dren

What kind of photos do elves take?
Elfies

What's a snowman's favourite food?
Chili dogs

Why did the snowman name his dog Frost?
Because frostbites

What's a dinosaur's least favourite reindeer?
Comet

How do Christmas trees get their email?
They log-on

Why did the eggnog go to school?
To get a eggucation

What did Luke Skywalker say after he planted a Christmas tree farm?
May the forest be with you

Why did the Christmas tree fail the algebra test?
It was stumped

What was the Christmas tree's favourite subject at school?
Treegonomotree

Which month does a Christmas tree hate?
Sep-timber

What do you call an elf who tells jokes?
A real Christmas card

How many elves does it take to change a light bulb?
Ten. One to change the lightbulb and
nine to stand on one another's shoulders

What is Santa's primary language?
North Polish

What did the wise men say after they offered up their
gifts of gold and frankincense?
Wait, there's myrrh

How can Santa deliver presents during a thunderstorm?
His sleigh is flown by raindeer

What is white and climbs up a mountain?
A homesick avalanche

What's an Ig?
A snow house without a loo

What did the squirrel go and see on Christmas Eve?
The Nutcracker

What kind of drink does Santa Claus give to naughty children?
Coal-a

Which of Santa Claus' friends is the most chill?
Jack Frost.

What does a Christmas tree farm, Christmas dinner and a hair salon all have in common?
Trimmings

Santa went to the Doctors with a problem
Doctor: What seems to be the problem?
Santa: I seem to have a mince pie stuck up my bottom!
Doctor: Well you're in luck,
I've got just the cream for that!

Two snowmen in a field, one turned to the other and said
"I don't know about you but I can smell carrots"

Did you know that Santa's not allowed to
go down chimneys this year?
It was declared unsafe
by the Elf and Safety Commission.

If you like Christmas so much...
Why don't you merry it?

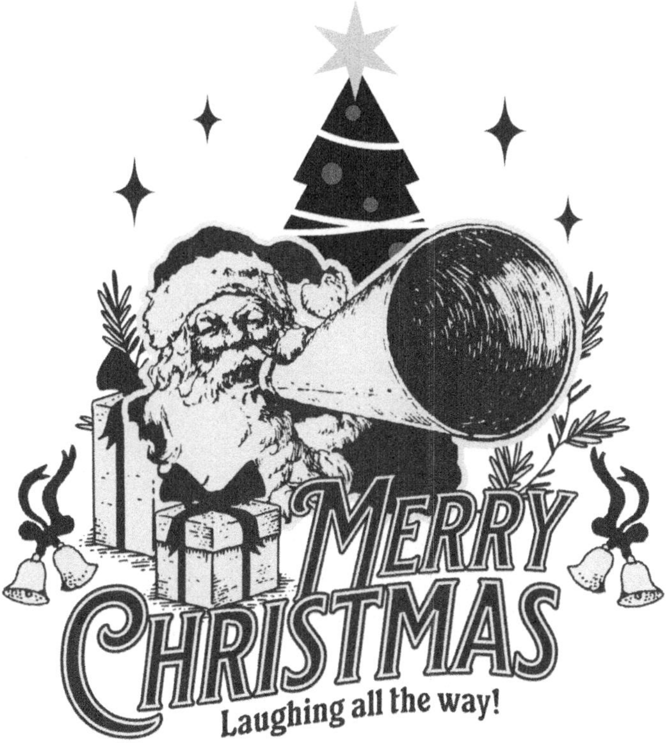
MERRY
CHRISTMAS
Laughing all the way!

Printed in Great Britain
by Amazon